Ian Sowers

The Sedan

DELTA Publishing

You can listen to *The Sedan* using the free DELTA Augmented app – you'll also find fun interactive activities!

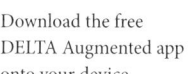

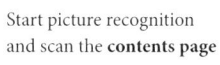

Download the free DELTA Augmented app onto your device	Start picture recognition and scan the **contents page**	Download files and use them now or save them for later

Apple and the Apple logo are trademarks of Apple Inc., registered in the US and other countries. App Store is a service mark of Apple Inc. | Google Play and the Google Play logo are trademarks of Google Inc.

1st edition   1 ⁵⁴³²¹ | 2027 26 25 24 23

All rights reserved. No part of this publication may be reproduced, stored in a retrieval system, or transmitted, in any form or by any means, electronic, mechanical, photocopying, recording, or otherwise, without prior written permission from the publisher.

Delta Publishing, 2022
www.deltapublishing.co.uk

© Ernst Klett Sprachen GmbH, Rotebühlstraße 77, 70178 Stuttgart, 2022

Author: Ian Sowers
Editor: Kate Baade
Annotations and activities: Megan Roderick

Cover and layout: Andreas Drabarek, Eva Lettenmayer
Illustrations: Harald Ardeias
Design: Datagroup int, Timisoara
Cover picture: Harald Ardeias
Printing and binding: Plump Druck & Medien GmbH, Rheinbreitbach

ISBN 978-3-12-501161-8

Contents

Chapter 1	6
Chapter 2	9
Chapter 3	17
Chapter 4	25
Chapter 5	34
Chapter 6	42
Chapter 7	51
Chapter 8	60
Chapter 9	72
Activities	76
Build your vocabulary	84
Find out more	90
Answer key	92

Abbreviations

sb   somebody
sth   something

Images:
4 123RF.com (Vadim Sazhniev), Nidderau; **90** 123RF.com (Chornii Yevhenii), Nidderau; **91** 123RF.com (Oleksandr Pupko), Nidderau

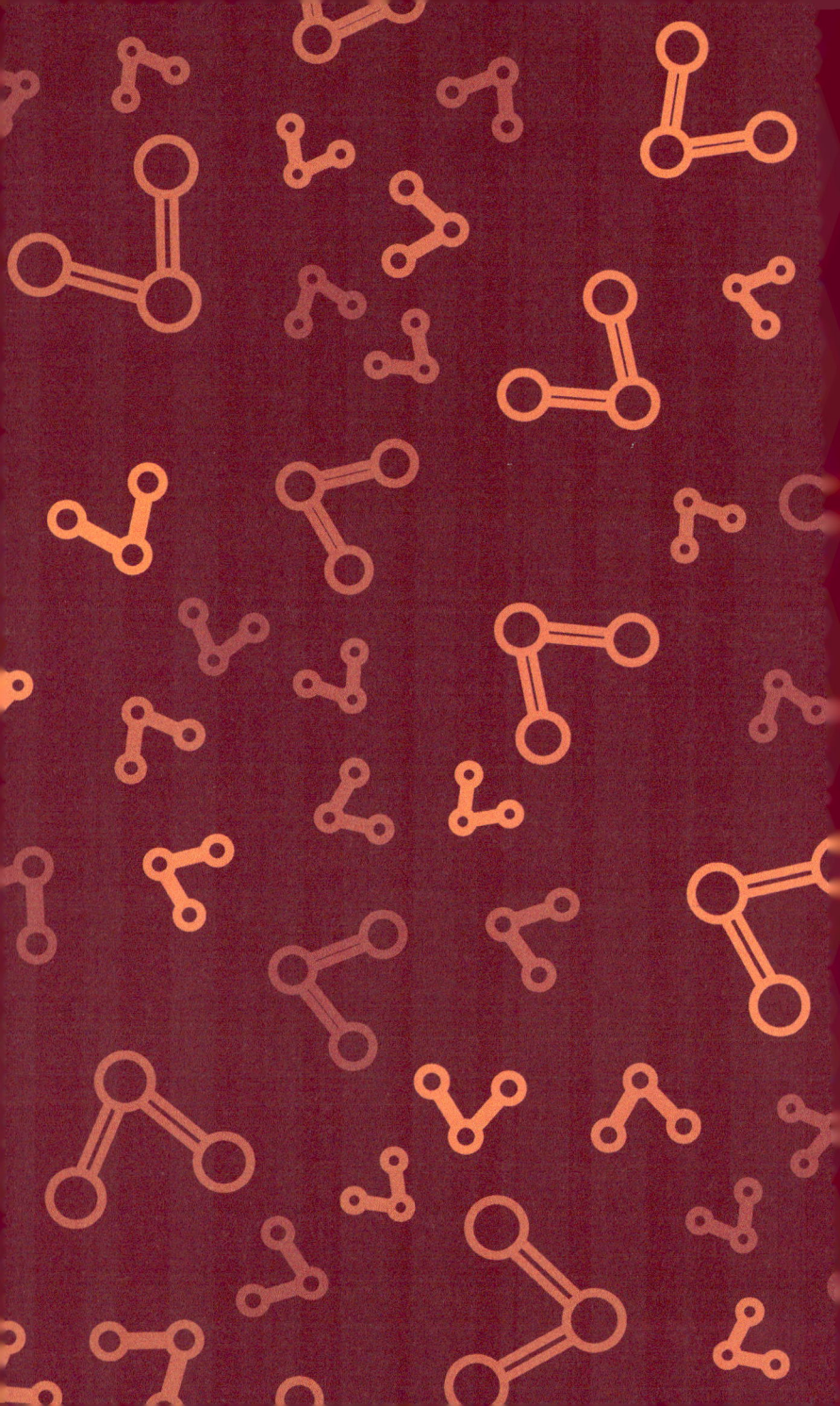

Before you start

1. What vocabulary would you associate with reading books about crime or thriller stories? Write words in your own language and in English.

words about crime	
My first language	English

2. What are some of the ways which a writer might use in order to create suspense? Think about a crime novel you have read and make a list.

_____
_____
_____
_____
_____

3. When you read *The Sedan*, think about what the writer is doing to create suspense and compare your findings with the list you made in Question 3. Add any other ways you find to your list.

Chapter 1

They moved slowly toward the farmhouse from the road, cell phone flashlights searching the ground for clear spots to place their feet. The moon was out and full, and the sky was bright. But the farmhouse yard was filled with tall pines, and the air was murky. The farmhouse was dark, but that didn't mean no one was inside, and they didn't want to step on a twig or a dry leaf and give themselves away.

On the west side of the house, toward the back, there was a small staircase that led up to what they thought was probably the entrance to a kitchen. There were two large, uncurtained windows there as well so they could get a look inside. Back in the car, they had decided to head in that direction instead of approaching the front. They thought they'd be less exposed.

---

23 **murky** gloomy, not light enough to see well – 24 **twig** small branch of a tree –
28 **uncurtained** without any curtains – 31 **exposed** *(here)* easily seen or visible

Halfway across the front yard, they turned toward the west side – and suddenly the yard was filled with light. A half dozen floodlights attached to the front of the house had suddenly come to life, and the murk was replaced by the equivalent of broad daylight. They froze, hoping that the lights had been triggered by motion detectors and not turned on manually by a living breathing human being who had actually seen them.

And then they saw the dog.

It had been standing on the front porch the entire time, concealed by the gloom. Now they saw it clearly, a large German Shepherd. Standing at attention, staring at them.

They looked at each other, the same question in their eyes: *What do we do now?*

> What are the people here trying to do?

> What two things happened to make them stop?

Think about it…

> How does the author set the scene for a mystery/crime story?

> What do you think will happen next?

---

4 **equivalent** sth that seems the same as sth else – 5 **to trigger** to cause sth, e.g. an alarm or lights, to start working – 6 **motion detector** a type of alarm that is set off by movement – 6 **manually** physically, by hand – 9 **porch** a small area at the entrance to a building covered by a roof – 10 **concealed** hidden from view – 10 **gloom** darkness

Chapter 2

Five days before…

Linda walked in without knocking, dropped her purse on the floor next to the front door, then moved directly to the living room. Stopping on the threshold, she smiled at her friends. They all smiled back except Shaun, whose eyes did not leave his phone, to acknowledge her arrival.

"Did you walk up here?" Wanda asked.

"Of course she walked up here," Shaun said snidely, still not looking up.

Linda and Hall exchanged a look. Neither of them took Shaun too seriously.

Wanda and their host Christa were stretched out on the couch in opposite directions, heads at either end, feet in the middle, almost touching. Hall was on a loveseat set at an angle to the couch, half of the loveseat empty, anticipating Linda's arrival. Shaun was in an armchair, facing the group but at a bit of a distance.

This was how it always was. This was normal.

Will I miss it? she suddenly wondered, and not for the first time.

"Did you see my Story?" Hall asked as she sat down next to him. She held out a hand; he kissed it.

"It's been a minute," she said. "Of course I saw your Story."

There were four champagne flutes on the coffee table, containing various amounts of an orangish fluid. Mimosas. They had started without her. Fair enough: she was late.

"Thanks for the photo credit," Linda said sarcastically.

"Do you really want to be known as someone who takes pictures of people in cars?" Hall asked.

Linda shrugged, then made a face conceding the point.

---

2 **purse** *(US Eng)* handbag – 4 **threshold** the entrance of a room – 6 **to acknowledge** to pay attention to, to take notice of – 8 **snidely** meanly – 25 **mimosa** a cocktail made of champagne and orange juice – 30 **to concede the point** to agree with sth that has been said

Rather than ask what photo they were talking about, Wanda and Christa picked up their phones. Who knew what Shaun was looking at.

"Hashtag 'get a room'?" Wanda said.

"Don't click it," Christa warned, then she asked, "Is that my street?"

"Your street?" Hall teased. "The street. Is there any other street up the hill?"

"Who are they?" Wanda asked.

Shaun finally looked up. "What are you talking about?"

"Check Hall's Insta," Christa said.

"I don't follow Hall on Instagram."

"It's true," Hall confirmed.

"He doesn't follow any of us," Linda added.

"I follow you," Wanda informed Shaun, sounding wounded.

Shaun lowered his phone to address his friends.

"I see all of you all the time," he pointed out. "Why do I need to follow you on Instagram?"

13 **to confirm** to say that sth is true or has been decided – 15 **wounded** hurt *(here)* emotionally

His friends looked at each other, and nodded. Satisfied, they moved on to the car.

"It's old," Christa said.

"Too old for this hill," Linda pointed out. Having seen the photo already, she and Hall were watching the others.

"And it's brown," Wanda said. "There are brown cars?"

"Is no one going to send me the pic?" Shaun asked the room.

"My Insta's public," Hall said.

Shaun glared at Hall, who laughed and looked at Linda, who laughed and said, "A lot of work, we know."

A few seconds later, Shaun said, "It's a sedan. Probably fifteen years old."

"What are they doing inside?" Wanda asked. She was always asking things.

"Probably what they used to do on this hill twenty years ago," Hall said.

They all smiled – even Shaun. They all knew.

This hill had once been covered in trees. Now it was covered in houses.

For decades before Linda and her friends were born, relatively rich and relatively poor lived side by side in relatively similar houses. There were signs that some people were better off than others – better cars, better clothes, longer and more extravagant vacations – but everyone was at the same elevation, shoulder to shoulder. It was a community defined and determined by location and therefore shared concerns, rather than wealth.

The hill to the east – like the lake to the west – was a feature, a bit of nature to be admired and enjoyed. There were ample trails to hike on, clearings for picnics, and an ungated, unguarded access road that spiraled up the hill to its treeless top. Residents

---

11 **sedan** a classic 4-door car which has separate sections for the engine, the passengers and the luggage area – 23 **extravagant** *(here)* costing a lot of money – 24 **elevation** height *(here)* of a landscape – 25 **defined and determined** given its character – 26 **concern** problematic issue – 28 **ample** a large amount of – 29 **clearing** an area without any trees – 30 **access road** a road that leads to a partiuclar business or group of houses

of the town could drive up there and enjoy a view of their homes, and the lake beyond. Or they could drive up there and make out.

And in fact that is what the hill was famous for years. It was Make Out Hill, the place where teens who could drive went before, after or instead of dates, to engage in a bit of amorous activity. It was an unwritten rule that only a certain number of cars could fit at the top. When that number was reached, cars would park along the access road at discrete intervals.

Then one day, two groups looked at the Hill and saw money, and shortly thereafter, a third group looked at the Hill and saw esteem.

The first of the first two groups was made up of people who wanted the trees; the second was made up of people who wanted to build and sell houses. The first two teamed up and convinced the third that they deserved a community more consistent with their achievements, an elevated community with a view.

This third group was crucial because in order to tear down its trees and build houses, the Hill would have to be re-zoned. And because this third group was rich and influential – and included several members of the town's government – the Hill was re-zoned.

"Maybe it's nostalgia," Hall suggested.

"Maybe they used to drive their crappy sedan up here back in the day?" Shaun asked.

"Maybe," Christa said. "And now my crappy house is here."

In fact, Christa's house had been built just off the edge of the treeless top. Perhaps unsurprisingly, it was the deputy mayor whose house had secured pride of place.

"I wonder if any of us were conceived in a car on this hill," Wanda said.

---

2 **to make out** to engage in romantic activity – 5 **to engage in** to be involved in –
5 **amorous** showing love or romantic feelings – 8 **discrete** separated by a certain distance –
11 **esteem** admiration – 17 **crucial** essential, very important – 21 **nostalgia** a sad feeling of trying to recover the past – 22 **crappy** *(slang)* awful, in a bad condition – 27 **to secure** to gain, to get – 27 **pride of place** the best position – 28 **to be conceived** the moment when a woman becomes pregnant with a child

"Oh," Linda gasped.

"Let's not wonder about that," Hall advised.

"No," Linda said, pivoting toward Hall. "Let's wonder about why you know nothing about my dress."

They were seniors, it was June, and prom was a week away. Shaun was boycotting the event, a stance enabled by the fact that no girl existed who would say yes if he asked her to go with him. Christina, who was performing in the upcoming school play, was going with one of her fellow actors, a boy none of them knew. Wanda was going with the boy she'd been vaguely dating for the last several years, another Hill-dweller who none of them really liked, not even Wanda. And Linda was going with Hall.

"What am I supposed to know about your dress?" he asked.

"The color?"

"Why?"

Realizing something, Linda slid backward into her end of the loveseat, away from Hall. Her mouth was agape, but she was smiling. Hall raised his eyebrows and widened his eyes, anticipating her next words.

"You don't have a tux," she said.

"I'm going tomorrow!" he exclaimed.

"And what do you think they're going to have for you tomorrow?" Linda wanted to know.

"A tux?"

"In your size? With a tie and cummerbund that match the color of my dress? Less than a week before prom?"

"I am optimistic." He waved his mimosa glass in the air, which seemed to remind Linda about something.

"Why do I not have a mimosa?" she asked the room.

"Because you didn't make yourself a mimosa," Christa answered.

---

3 **to pivot** to turn around quickly – 6 **to boycott** to deliberately not attend a particular event – 6 **stance** attitude, opinion – 6 **to enable** to make sth possible – 17 **agape** wide open – 20 **tux** short for tuxedo *(US English)*, dinner jacket – 25 **cummerbund** a waist sash, often made of silk, worn with a tuxedo on very formal occasions

Linda stood up and went into the kitchen. Hall let a moment pass, then he stood up and followed her.

Unlike the living room – which was moody, almost gloomy – the kitchen was brightly lit. Linda moved around the kitchen island, opened the fridge, and pulled out an opened bottle of cava.

"Sorry I flaked," Hall said as he entered. He stopped on the opposite end of the island and leaned against it on his forearms.

"It's alright," Linda said, setting the cava on the island. Then she went back in for the orange juice. "I'm not sure either one of us is taking this seriously."

Hall moved around the island to the cupboard where the champagne flutes were kept. He pulled one out and set it next to the cava.

"I'm taking it seriously," he said, taking the orange juice from her. "Mostly OJ, right?"

"Ha ha," she said drily. Then she picked up the cava and nearly filled the flute, stopping just half an inch from the rim. "You can top me off."

He topped her off. The cava turned orange.

"There," Linda said. "Now it's healthy."

She picked up her glass and took a sip.

"Healthi*er*," Hall said, stressing the last syllable. Then he added, "Maybe."

"So," Linda began. "What time am I picking you up tomorrow?"

"Why? What are we doing?"

"Oh my god," Linda said, rolling her eyes. "You've got the memory of a chimp."

"Better than the memory of a bee," Hall said with a shrug.

She punched him gently in the shoulder, then exclaimed, "We need to get you a tux!"

---

7 **to flake** (US Eng) to fail or neglect to do sth alread agreed on – 30 **shrug** a movement of the shoulders up and down to suggest that you don't really care

"Ah, the tux."

"Yeah, apparently I'm spending my Sunday trying to track one down."

> How would you describe the Hill's status now?

> Why was Linda not exactly pleased with Hall?

Think about it...

> Think about the place where you live. Have certain areas changed in importance and/or respectability over the years? Why?

> Finishing your high school education and going to college or moving away from home is a significant change in a young person's life. Make a list of some of the advantages and disadvantages of leaving home.

---

2 **to track sth down** to try and find sth

Chapter 3

Hall's house was about halfway up the Hill, on the side that they referred to as 'the back'. Instead of a view of the town and the lake, it had one of the mountains about 40 miles to the east. The mountains were impressive, but it was considered the 'lesser' view, which meant the houses on the back of the Hill were cheaper. Certainly more expensive than the houses in town, but cheap for the Hill.

A set of stone steps led up to Hall's elevated front yard. He was sitting on them looking at his phone when Linda pulled up in her mother's convertible. It was a warm and sunny day, so she had the top down, even though the wind would make a mess of her long black hair. Whatever. They were running an errand, not going out.

"You ready?" Linda asked as Hall approached the car.

"No," he replied. "I hate shopping."

---

26 **convertible** a car with a roof that can be removed or folded down – 28 **to run an errand** to do a necessary chore outside the house

"And I hate shopping with people who hate shopping. Get in and let's get this over with."

Linda had decided that their first stop would be Southeast Village – not because it was anybody's favorite shopping mall, but precisely because it wasn't. Built in the 1970s on pastureland southeast of town, its developers had predicted that as the town grew, it would grow toward them, making the mall's location ideal. As it turned out, they had predicted wrong. The town had grown, but in every other direction, which meant that it was inconvenient for almost everybody. It didn't help that few improvements had been made to the building over the years, and as a result it looked and felt a bit shabby.

"Our Story got some weird views," Hall said, squinting at his phone.

"Those weird porn things?" Linda asked as she navigated the car down the Hill.

"No, that's real world weird, but internet normal. I mean internet weird."

"Aha."

"I got three views from accounts that I'm not connected to in any way," he explained. "I don't follow them, they don't follow me, and it looks like they don't know anybody I know. Their usernames are just random letters and punctuation. Their accounts are public, but they've posted nothing, not even profile pics."

Now Linda furrowed her brow. "None of them has a profile pic?"

"Nope," Hall confirmed. "None."

"So it's like the same thing three times."

"Yep."

At the bottom of the Hill, Linda turned right toward Southeast Village. Another misfortune the mall had suffered involved the

---

10 **inconvenient** causing problems or difficulties – 12 **shabby** not well looked after – 13 **to squint** to look at sb/sth with difficulty – 23 **random** having no particular meaning or association; chosen by chance – 26 **to furrow your brow** to frown – 31 **misfortune** sth unlucky that happens

proposed freeway interchange, where the north-south interstate was to meet the east-west. The same developers who had believed that the town would grow toward them also believed that the interchange would be built on their doorstep. In the end, no interchange was ever built, which not only made transferring from one freeway to the other complicated, it also meant no freeway route to Southeast Village. Furthermore, the route by car was by no means straightforward.

Linda turned on the GPS.

"So what do you think is going on?" she asked Hall.

"Well, you can't view Stories if you're not logged in."

"This is true," Linda confirmed. "I have tried this. It does not work."

Hall looked over at Linda, grinning.

Linda sighed dramatically and said, "Shut up. And carry on."

Hall laughed and continued.

"So, somebody – well, three somebodies. Three somebodies knew about the picture and wanted to see it, but they didn't want me to know who they were, so they created Instagram accounts so they could look at it."

Hall looked over at Linda to gauge her reaction. They were traveling at a good clip now, and her thick, black hair was a tornado all over her head. She looked at him quizzically. He forgot what he had been talking about.

"Your hair," he said, sounding almost despairing.

"I know," she said. "And I don't care. We're going to Southeast Village."

The vast parking lot that surrounded the mall was sparsely occupied, so they were able to park close to the front entrance. The sun had gone behind a cloud, resulting in a grayness that

---

1 **interchange** where two or more main roads cross – 1 **interstate** *(US Eng)* motorway – 4 **on your doorstep** very near – 5 **to transfer** *(here)* to move from one main road to another – 8 **straightforward** *(here)* easy to navigate – 21 **to gauge** to try and guess or understand – 22 **at a good clip** at a high speed – 23 **tornado** a type of windstorm that moves in a circle – 28 **sparsely occupied** *(here)* with only a few other cars there

seemed fitting. Walking toward the edifice, Hall wondered aloud why none of the funds the town had received from the federal government had been allocated to sprucing up the mall a bit.

"It's not really what the town is anymore," he observed, "but it's what the town was."

"You're a strange boy, Hall," Linda said as she opened the front door and stepped inside.

The mall was cavernous, the ceilings high. There were other people there, but that didn't prevent their footsteps from echoing off the tile floors as they marched to the information desk. The tuxedo shop, they found out, was at the complete other end of the mall, so far away from where they were currently standing that Linda briefly considered going back to the car and driving around. But she quickly changed her mind.

"We both need the steps," Linda told Hall.

"Speak for yourself," he replied.

They took their time walking through the unfamiliar mall, taking in their surroundings. Most of the stores were ones you'd find in other malls, although the big ones were missing. Then there were a number of stores neither of them had heard of, plus more than a few vacancies. A lot of stores were advertising sales.

"How is this still here?" Linda asked.

"Sheer force of will?" Hall suggested.

They turned a corner and saw the tuxedo shop in front of them at the end of the corridor. There was just one person inside, and it looked like she worked there: she was behind the counter.

"Empty," Linda said.

"Which means what?"

"Either they've got all of the tuxes. Or none of them."

---

1 **fitting** suitable – 1 **edifice** a large building – 3 **to allocate** to put to a particular purpose or use – 3 **to spruce sth up** to make sth look nicer and smarter – 8 **cavernous** huge (of an interior) – 8 **ceiling** the top inside surface of a room – 18 **to take sth in** to absorb, to appreciate sth – 18 **surroundings** the particular place or area sb/sth is in – 21 **vacancies** empty/unused shopping outlets or stores

Entering the store, Linda immediately realized they both knew the girl behind the counter.

"Hey, Beth!" she said. "I didn't know you worked here."

Beth, a fellow senior, was a good friend of Christa's and was also working on the school play. She didn't live on the Hill. She and Christa had met when they were small, when Christa's family had lived in town, and they had stayed close.

"Linda!" Beth came out from behind the counter, smiling warmly. "Hall!"

Linda and Hall couldn't help but smile back. Beth was genuinely one of the nicest people either of them had ever met, despite having had more than a few curveballs thrown at her.

"What are you all doing down here?" Beth asked.

"We're here because Hall is an idiot," Linda stated flatly.

Hall pursed his lips and nodded.

Beth laughed and said, "I'm sure that's not true."

"He's my date for prom," Linda elaborated, "and he hasn't got a tux yet."

"Oh alright," Beth said, giving Hall a look. "So maybe… yeah."

"Beth!" Hall exclaimed, looking scandalized.

Beth laughed again, harder this time.

"Come on," she said, taking Hall by the shoulder. "Let's get you fitted."

Beth told them she hadn't had a prom customer in weeks: it was all summer weddings now. But their prom business had been light, as usual – and as Linda had hoped – and so they had more than a few tuxes available for the upcoming weekend.

Hall stood in the middle of the store – arms extended, legs slightly parted – as Beth took his measurements. Linda sat on a padded bench off to one side, scrutinizing the photo of the sedan.

---

12 **curveball** a difficult or unexpected life situation or event – 14 **flatly** without showing emotion – 15 **to elaborate** to explain sth further – 20 **scandalized** very shocked – 28 **extended** *(here)* stretched out to either side – 30 **to scrutinize** to look carefully at sth/sb in detail

"Can you see anything?" Hall asked as Beth circled him with her tape measure.

"Nothing," Linda said. "I mean, you can see what they're doing, more or less. But no faces."

"And the plate?"

"Nope."

"You're zooming in?"

"Yes."

"All the way in?"

Linda lowered her phone and glared at him.

"No, just some of the way in," she said drily. "Because I want to do this badly."

Beth stood upright and stepped in front of Hall.

"Alright," she said. "You can put your arms down."

"Oh thank god," Hall said with a sigh, letting his arms drop.

Beth turned to Linda and asked, "So what color's your dress?"

"Maya blue," Linda replied, suddenly digging through her purse.

"That's very specific," Hall observed.

"<u>You're</u> very specific," Linda shot back.

Hall gave her a confused look. She shrugged.

"There's a number…" Linda said, still searching her purse.

But Beth was already on her phone.

"So, a bright light blue," she said, then she looked up at Linda with a smile. "We can match that."

On the long walk back to the front entrance, Linda asked Hall if he had made screenshots of the weird accounts. He said he had, then he asked, "Why?"

Looking uneasy, Linda shrugged.

What reasons are given for the decline in popularity of the Southeast Village shopping mall?

What does Linda mean when she says to Hall: 'We both need the steps'?

Think about it...

How careful are you generally about Internet security? Is it something that worries you and your friends?

What advice would you give to someone just starting to use social media?

Chapter 4

Will I miss it?

That question again, this time entering Linda's head as she walked through the high school parking lot, being greeted warmly by almost everyone she passed, even people she didn't know that well.

Will I miss it?

Suddenly Wanda was next to her, already looking harried and confused.

"Did Hall get his tux?" she asked.

"Just barely," Linda replied. "We had to go to Southeast Village."

"Wow."

"Mm-hmm."

Shaun drove past them. They waved and smiled. He looked back at them with a flat expression.

"Why are we friends with him?" Wanda asked.

"We're trying to break him," Linda replied.

It was 7:45. They still had fifteen minutes to pass by their lockers and get to their homeroom. According to science, they shouldn't have even been awake yet. Yet here they were.

"How's it going?" Linda asked, because she knew it wasn't going well.

Wanda sighed and said, "I don't think I'm going to make it."

Like all of them, Wanda didn't necessarily want to go to university, but she expected to. Or at least she had expected to. But then all but one of the universities she had applied to had turned her down. And the one that had accepted her – her safety school – had accepted her conditionally. If she didn't get a 3.25 grade point average this quarter, their offer would be revoked.

"Why not?" Linda asked.

"I'm failing Life Skills."

"Oh no."

---

7 **harried** worried – 26 **to turn sb down** *(here)* to reject an application – 27 **conditionally** depend on getting good grades – 28 **to revoke** to officially change a decision or an offer

Life Skills, unlike most of their courses, was designed to prepare students for actual life. Things like managing your finances, time management, and first aid. And it was an elective: Wanda had chosen to take it, and now she was failing it.

They'd almost reached the end of the parking lot. Linda looked up – Wanda was tall – and saw that her friend's eyes were watery.

Linda stopped her and said, "Let's have lunch together, alright? At the field? Just you and me?"

"Alright."

The field was on a treeless ridge above the football field, opposite the school. It was technically on campus, but it took some time to get there. Until the school decided what horrible use to make of it – a second parking lot seemed likely – it was a nice, grassy place to have lunch, weather permitting.

Linda and Wanda were sitting cross-legged on a blanket Linda had retrieved from her car, eating a lunch they had pieced together

---

3 **elective** a subject or part of a course that sb chooses to take – it is not compulsory –
32 **to retrieve** to get sth from somewhere

with items from the vending machines outside the cafeteria. Not exactly healthy, or even filling, but it would do for today.

"Could I bribe him?" Wanda asked.

They were talking about Mr. Adams, the Life Skills teacher.

"Does that happen in real life?" Linda asked back, looking skeptical.

"Linda," Wanda began, looking almost offended, "I'm the naive one, not you."

Linda raised her hands and nodded.

"Fair enough," she said. "But maybe before you break the law–"

"Is bribing a teacher against the law?" Wanda interrupted.

Normalcy restored, Linda thought, *and in record time.*

"If giving them isn't," she said, "accepting them certainly is."

"Okay."

"So maybe before you break the law," Linda repeated, "how about just talking to him? Maybe there's some extra work you could do to improve your grade?"

"Do I have time to do extra work?"

The end of the year – and the end of high school – was just a couple of weeks away.

"I think you need to talk to him," Linda said, adding, "I'll go with you."

Wanda sighed heavily, and again there were tears in her eyes. She uncrossed her legs and lay back on the blanket.

"It's so confusing," she said, her eyes on the lone cloud in the sky.

Linda took her hand.

"When I think about September," Wanda continued, "I see me at university. When I try to see me somewhere else, I can't. If I'm not at university in September, where am I?"

---

1 **vending machine** a machine where you can buy snacks and drinks – 2 **filling** when food satisfies your hunger – 3 **to bribe** to offer money in return for a favor – 6 **skeptical** doubtful – 7 **offended** shocked, hurt, upset – 7 **naive** lacking experience of life – 12 **normalcy** sb's usual or normal state – 12 **to restore** to bring back to a previous state – 25 **lone** single

It'll be okay, Linda wanted to say, but she didn't know if that was true. Not only had she been wondering about her past lately, she had also been wondering about her future.

Her place at university was secure – she'd been accepted by her first choice and hadn't even had a safety school – and she knew what she wanted to study. But what kind of world would she be entering when university ended? Everything seemed to be moving in the wrong direction.

She turned her head so she could see the lake-facing side of the Hill in the distance. She couldn't exactly see it, but she knew she was more or less looking at her house.

Everything. Moving in the wrong direction. And somehow she was both a victim and part of the problem.

She squeezed Wanda's hand.

Then a notification on her phone caught her eye. Instagram. She picked up her phone to check it. Instagram was bothering her lately.

She had a new follower request. Someone named Mary Jessel. She looked at Mary Jessel's profile, scrolled through her photos. Nothing seemed familiar, not the places where the photos had been taken, not the people in them.

Then Linda noticed that Mary Jessel's username was not maryjessel. It was something completely different, not even close. Not even words, really.

She looked over and saw that Wanda was squinting at her.

"What?" Wanda asked.

"We're going to talk to Mr. Adams, right?"

Wanda made a face, then reluctantly nodded.

"Okay," Linda said. "I need to talk to Hall."

"Yep," Hall confirmed. "That's one of them: alfj.juk.bugds."

---

14 **to squeeze** to hold sth tightly – 15 **notification** *(on phone)* a message –
28 **reluctantly** not really wanting to do sth

The three of them were standing in the hallway, students streaming past them in both directions, just minutes before lunch was going to end.

"One of what?" Wanda asked.

Linda had tried to explain the whole thing to Wanda on their way to meet Hall. To no avail, apparently.

"One of the random accounts that looked at the picture of that sedan," Linda said.

Hall was looking at the account on his own phone.

"Except now it's got a name and a profile pic and posts," he added.

"What's the name?" Wanda asked.

"Mary Jessel."

And a few seconds later, they were all looking at it.

"All the photos were posted today," Wanda said.

"Yep," Hall confirmed.

"They probably aren't theirs," Wanda continued. "They probably reposted them and the captions from some other account."

Wanda looked up. Linda and Hall were both looking at her.

"There are apps," she said.

Linda and Hall both lowered their phones.

"No point in looking at them then," Hall said.

The hallway was almost empty now, but none of them had noticed.

"So, some random person opens an account to look at your Story," Linda recapped, "then adds names and posts and sends me a friend request." She finished with a question. "So, they can look at my posts?"

"Is there any way this person could possibly know that you took the photo in my Story?" Hall asked.

"Did you tell anyone?"

"No," Hall replied. "I don't know why I would've."

---

2 **to stream past** to go past in a crowd – 6 **to no avail** in vain, without success –
17 **caption** a short text that goes with a photo or post – 26 **to recap** to repeat

"So, the only people who know," Linda said, "are the five of us who were at Christa's on Saturday. And whoever Mary Jessel is?"

Now it was just the three of them in the hallway. They stood there in silence, wearing puzzled expressions. Then the bell announcing the start of fourth period rang, and they all snapped out of it. And with one last glance at each other, they hurried off in three different directions.

The school day had ended, and once again Linda and Wanda were in the field, sitting cross legged on Linda's blanket. This time, however, they were joined by Hall, who was lying on his side in the unmown grass, propped up on an elbow. On the football field down below, they could see the lacrosse team practicing for their final match.

"Okay," Hall began, "before we pursue some scary theory that potentially involves being betrayed by one of our friends–"

"Or Shaun," Linda interjected.

"Or Shaun. Let's consider a more likely although also kind of scary theory: old perverts."

Linda nodded, willing to hear him out. It was the internet after all.

"Some old pervert starts an Instagram account so that he can do some perverting," Hall continued. "He stumbles across my account and scrolls through my friends, looking for some pretty young girls to be creepy with, and that's when he finds you."

"My profile pic is Lala Gonzalez from 'School Rumble,'" Linda pointed out.

"There is a resemblance."

"But old pervert wouldn't know that."

"He's a hopeful old pervert."

"I didn't get a friend request," Wanda said, sounding doleful.

---

5 **to snap out of it** to suddenly come out of a period of deep thought – 11 **unmown** not recently cut – 11 **to prop up** to lean on – 12 **lacrosse** a team sport played on grass – 14 **to pursue** *(here)* to find out more about, to follow up – 15 **potentially** possibly (in the future) – 15 **to be betrayed by** to be hurt by sb who is not loyal to you – 21 **to stumble across** to find sth by chance – 23 **creepy** showing worrying and inappropriate behavior – 26 **resemblance** when sb/sth looks similar to sb/sth else – 29 **doleful** sad

Linda and Hall looked at her.

"Should I be offended?" she asked.

"No," they replied, almost in unison.

Linda turned back to Hall.

"Okay, but why did he start with your account?" she asked. "If he was looking for 'pretty young girls', why start with a boy?"

"That's because nice-looking young boys often have a lot of pretty young girls as friends, or at least as Instagram followers," Hall explained.

"Okay," Linda said, "but why did he start with your account?"

"You're hilarious," Hall sneered.

A buzzing sound attracted their attention. Linda's phone.

"It's Shaun," she said, looking at the screen.

She took the call and turned on the speaker.

"Hey," she said.

"Hey," Shaun said back. "You guys remember that sedan that was on the Hill?"

"Yeah," Linda said, "but what do you mean 'you guys'?"

"You and Hall and Wanda."

"How do you–?"

"I'm looking at you," he interrupted. "I'm over by the tennis courts."

They all turned and looked toward the tennis courts, which were above the football field between the school and the parking lot. They saw a figure sitting on a bench. The figure raised a hand and waved.

"Sure we remember the sedan," Linda said. "We were just talking about it, sort of."

"Did you see the story about the car they found at that rest area?" Shaun asked.

---

3 **in unison** together at the same time – 11 **hilarious** very funny – 11 **to sneer** to say sth in an unpleasant or joking manner – 21 **to interrupt** to start speaking while sb else is already saying sth

Linda looked at Hall and Wanda. They picked up their phones and started searching.

"We're checking," Linda said. "But what about it?"

"It's that sedan."

"What?"

"The car they found is that sedan," he said. "With a broken window and blood on the front passenger seat."

> What exactly was Wanda's problem relating to getting into university?

> What does Linda suggest that Wanda should do?

Think about it...

> Many young people feel uncertainty about the future. What is the best way of dealing with that, do you think?

> Technology is a powerful tool these days in helping to solve crimes. Write down a few ways in which you think it can help.

Chapter 5

They didn't even consider asking Shaun to join them in the field; they knew he wouldn't. Instead they packed up Linda's blanket, walked down and across the football field, and then climbed up to the tennis courts. Wanda, exhausted from the journey, sat down next to Shaun on the bench, while Linda and Hall remained standing.

They'd all read the story now. A brown sedan had been discovered abandoned in the parking lot of a rest area along the freeway about 100 miles east of town, on the other side of the mountains. The front passenger-side window had been completely smashed out, presumably from the inside as very little broken glass had been found inside the car. There was also, however, very little glass found on the ground outside the car, leading investigators to conclude that the window had been broken in a different location.

---

27 **presumably** seeming to be true – 30 **investigator** an offical examining the facts of a crime – 30 **to conclude** to find as a result

A quantity of blood had been discovered on the front passenger seat as well as on the inside and the outside of the door. It was unclear if the blood and the broken window were connected. It also could not be determined if the amount of blood present definitively indicated a death or simply a severe injury.

It had not yet been confirmed that the blood was human. However, because steps had been taken to conceal the identity of the sedan, investigators were operating on the assumption that the source of the blood was a person not an animal. There was nothing in the car – not just emptied of items that might be used to identify the owner, but emptied of everything – and the license plates had been removed. But most significantly, the VIN – vehicle identification number – on the dashboard had been filed away and was unreadable.

Like most rest areas in the state, this one had security cameras. However, the sedan had entered the parking lot in a blind spot, so investigators had no footage of it. Local authorities, in cooperation with state police, were asking anyone who had stopped at the rest area in the last 72 hours to get in touch.

"You're sure?" Hall asked Shaun.

"I'm pretty sure," Shaun replied.

"How can you be pretty sure?" Hall wanted to know.

When Shaun looked up from his phone to answer Hall, it was Linda his eyes landed on. She was looking at him intently, her lips a tight line.

"Are you okay?" he asked her.

"No," she answered bluntly.

Shaun shifted his gaze to Hall.

"First of all, it's the same make, model and color," Shaun continued, "and yeah, before you ask, there are probably

---

4 **to determine** to decide – 4 **present** being in a particular place – 4 **definitively** without any doubt – 5 **to indicate** to show or prove – 5 **severe** very serious – 7 **to conceal** to hide – 8 **assumption** belief that sth is true, without having proof – 13 **to file sth away** *(here)* to deliberately get rid of sth by cutting it away with a metal file – 17 **footage** video recording (from the cameras) – 27 **bluntly** directly, simply – 28 **to shift** to move

thousands of brown fifteen-year-old cars like this on the road right now. It was a very popular car."

"Yeah, but brown?" Wanda interjected.

"Technically I think it's sandalwood or dark taupe," Shaun said. He knew a lot about cars. "But yeah brown."

Wanda shrugged.

"So," Shaun went on, "the make, model and color made me pay attention, but it was three other things that made me pretty sure it's the same car. One, in the picture of the car on that news site, you can see that that car is missing its left rear hubcap. Now look at Linda's picture."

Linda and Hall immediately raised their phones. The car had been parked on the side of the road, facing downhill, and Linda had taken the picture just after she had passed it. The left rear wheel was the nearest wheel, and it was clearly missing a hubcap.

They both looked up at Shaun.

"No hubcap?" he asked them.

"No hubcap," Hall confirmed.

"Two, in Linda's pic, I remember a round sticker on the rear window that seemed to be intact. Maybe you can zoom in and see what it says. I couldn't on Instagram."

Almost in unison, Linda and Hall used a thumb and forefinger to zoom in.

"I can't," Hall said, shaking his head. He looked at Linda. "Can you? You've got the original."

"No, not really," she said. "Just some color – red and blue – and what might be a face?"

"Well it doesn't really matter," Shaun said. "On the other sedan, there *was* a sticker on the rear window, but someone removed most of it. Now there's just a white circle. Maybe it would've identified the owner so whoever left the car there tore it off."

---

3 **to interject** to interrupt sb – 10 **hubcap** the round metal cover in the middle of a wheel – 20 **intact** not damaged, complete – 29 **rear** *(here)* belonging to the back part of the vehicle – 31 **to identify** to discover who sb is

"And three?" Hall asked.

"The rear bumper," Shaun said. "It's newer than the car. It was replaced, relatively recently. That's a fifteen-year-old car, but that's not a fifteen-year-old bumper."

Linda and Hall were looking at their phones again, brows furrowed, squinting, unable to see what Shaun was talking about.

"Just trust me," he told them.

They lowered their phones.

"So, what do we do now?" Shaun wanted to know.

Wanda lowered her phone and asked, "What do we do about what?"

They all glanced at her screen. TikTok.

"Wanda," Shaun said, "this is probably a good time to be present."

"Are we still talking about that picture?"

"Some of us are." Shaun turned back to Linda and Hall. "So?"

"Do we have to <u>do</u> something?" Hall asked.

"This is just getting weirder," Linda said.

Now it was Shaun's turn to furrow his brow.

"What's getting weirder?" he asked.

Linda and Hall quickly explained the recent events on Instagram.

"Isn't that just an old pervert?" Shaun asked, still looking confused.

"My profile pic is an anime character," Linda said.

"Well then it's definitely an old pervert."

"Shaun."

"Linda?"

"What do <u>you</u> think we should do?"

Shaun, who had been leaning back, one arm hanging over the back of the bench, now sat up and leaned forward, his hands on his knees.

---

2 **bumper** a bar on the front and back of a car which helps to prevent damage to the car if hit – 3 **to replace** to change sth old for a newer version – 3 **relatively** quite – 8 **to lower** to put down

"I think," he said, "we should go to the police."

"And tell them what?" Linda asked.

"Tell them what we know."

"What do I know? A car that you say is the same car that was parked on the Hill. A couple of people were in the front seat making out, but I didn't see their faces. It was gross, so I took a photo, but you can't see anything in it. I can confirm that there was a brown sedan there, but that's it."

"The car was on the Hill. They probably don't know that. So you should tell them."

Shaun went in with her, to explain why he thought it was the same car. Linda told them her brief story and airdropped them the photo. The police told them they'd contact the relevant jurisdiction – the rest area was in a different county – and share with them the information that Linda and Shaun had provided. Then a decision would be made about whether or not to involve the state police.

When they came out, Hall was across the street, leaning on the hood of his car. After they told him what had happened, he asked, "So they're not involving the state police right away?"

"That's not surprising," Shaun said. "It isn't their case. But I don't care. We did our bit."

He took his keychain out and gave it a twirl.

"I'm off," he said. Then he turned and walked away toward his car, leaving Linda and Hall alone.

Hall looked at Linda. She was looking everywhere else but at him. He took one of her hands. She looked at him.

"You want to go for a walk?" he asked.

The sky was clear, and the evening was warm. It hadn't rained in weeks, which was unusual. The police station was near the lake, and so it was a short walk down to the waterfront park. It

---

6 **gross** disgusting – 12 **to airdrop** to transfer files between electronic gadgets wirelessly – 14 **jurisdiction** an area or a country with its own system of laws – 23 **to give sth a twirl** to spin sth around

wasn't quite the golden hour, but the light hitting them as they walked along the shore had a similar beauty.

Hall knew Linda well. They had met in junior high, after Hall's family had relocated from Georgia, and bonded almost immediately. They had similar senses of humor, and similar tastes, and instinct told them they had something even deeper in common. She'd made him feel welcome and brought him into her circle of friends, and they had been inseparable ever since. She was the first person he contacted every morning, and the last person she contacted at night. It was safe to say they needed each other.

Linda knew Hall well. She knew that, unlike everybody else, he had detected the recent shift in her mood, and that he was worried about her. She also knew that he wouldn't ask her about it outright, because he didn't like it when people did that with him. He would just create an opportunity like this one – an impromptu walk by the lake – and if she wanted to take advantage of it, she could.

"I'm not ready to talk about it," she said suddenly.

"Okay."

"Although it's not an 'it', really, it's two things."

To this, he offered no reply.

"It's not that I don't want to talk about it," she went on, "it's that I don't really know <u>how</u> to. The first thing makes me seem cold. The other thing makes me seem… unsympathetic. I feel like there's no way for me to talk about either thing without loathing myself."

"When you're ready to give it a try," Hall began, "let me know."

"Okay. But let me just ask you one thing."

"Shoot."

"We're both basically rich, right?"

---

4 **to bond** to develop a friendly relationship with sb, to feel close to sb – 8 **inseparable** extremely close (friends) – 13 **to detect** to discover, to notice – 15 **outright** directly – 17 **impromptu** unplanned – 25 **unsympathetic** uncaring – 26 **to loathe** to hate

"I would say that a lot of people would say that, yeah."

"Are you okay with it?" she asked.

Her eyes were on his face now, trying to read his reaction and anticipate what he was going to say. For the moment, however, he said nothing, so she went on.

"Because I'm not. Most of the people in this country worry about money. We don't. I never have. I can't even imagine what that feels like. It's been like that for hundreds of years, because that's basically how our system has always worked, but it's just getting worse and worse. And it's that same system that seems to enjoy making life hard for anyone who isn't a straight, white male, regardless of whether they have money or not."

"You sound like a Democrat," Hall said.

"No I don't. Do your parents vote?"

"Not really."

"Neither do mine. Because they know that it doesn't matter who's in charge. Democrat or Republican, they'll still be rich."

> What factors make it seem likely that the brown sedan was the scene of a crime?

> What two problems does Linda mention she has with 'the system'?

Think about it...

> Being rich and being poor have their own problems. What are some of them?

> Do you think that society will always be divided in this way? Why/Why not?

---

4 **to anticipate** to predict

Chapter 6

Linda had started talking and now she couldn't stop, so they found a spot in the grass next to the path and sat down. University was clear, she explained, but what about after that? Would she just take her degree and her wealth and become part of the system she loathed? Or would she set aside her privilege and work to get the world headed in the right direction?

"After, of course, letting your rich parents pay for your tuition and your room and board for four years," Hall pointed out.

"Now, see, that's one of the parts," Linda said.

"One of the parts that makes you loathe yourself?"

"Yes. Another part is when I imagine myself just finishing university, getting a good job, and doing absolutely nothing about anything."

"Would you actually do that?"

"Of course. I mean, I've been doing nothing most of my life. Pretending I'm something I'm not, playing the role of the

---

20 **wealth** a large amount of money or property – 21 **to set aside** to reject – 22 **to head** to move or go in a certain direction – 23 **tuition** education, teaching

traditional, inoffensive young rich person." Then she added, "You've been doing it too."

"I like to think that I am occasionally offensive."

"You know what I mean."

He did.

Then he said, "I know you're having a hard time, but you're basically telling yourself what you should do."

"Do something and start doing it now?" Linda said.

"That's why it's sometimes good to talk about stuff," Hall said. "You hear yourself."

"Hmm."

"So that's the thing you thought would make you seem unsympathetic," Hall said, then he asked, "What was the thing you thought would make you seem cold?"

Linda made a noise and looked across the lake. Now it really was the golden hour: everything was soft and red.

"I feel like I've spent my whole life up till now working hard on something that doesn't matter," she said, still looking at the lake.

"Something," Hall repeated. "Are we talking about your whole life up till now? Or something more specific?"

Still facing the lake, she looked over at him.

"Mainly the… relationships."

"Oh."

"Yeah."

"You're *cold*."

She hit him hard on the shoulder.

"Ouch," he said in an ironic tone. "Maybe you should be worrying about your lack of upper body strength."

"Pot kettle black."

"Okay. So *ice* cold."

"It's just that I spent all this time and emotion working on my relationships, caring about them. And in three months, we're all

---

1 **inoffensive** not likely to upset anyone – 27 **ironic** joking – 29 **the pot calling the kettle black** *(idiom)* don't criticize sb for a fault you have yourself

going to be in different places, connecting on social media like we do now with people we've never even met. It's like the only thing that really mattered was school."

"But are you going to miss school?"

"Hell no."

"Are you going to miss me?"

Will I miss it?

Suddenly Linda's eyes were heavy with tears.

"Oh god. Yes. You and Wanda and Christa. Even Shaun–"

"Don't get carried away."

"Okay."

Hall moved in a little bit closer and put an arm around her shoulders.

"If you're going to miss it," he said, "it mattered. Trying to convince yourself that it didn't matter to make splitting up easier isn't going to work."

"Is that what I'm doing?"

"Yeah, and that's what I did. Almost right away, when I realized that we were all going different places in the fall."

"Was that that weird week back in April?"

"Yeah, that was that weird week."

It was nearly dark now. The sun was out of sight behind the mountains.

"Is there any way for it not to suck?" she asked.

"Nope," Hall replied. "I think we just have to go through it."

When Linda got home, her parents were watching TV in the living room. They were on the sofa, her father sitting, her mother lying on her side with her head on his lap. They greeted her without looking away from the TV screen. She returned their greeting without stopping and climbed the stairs to her room.

In bed, just before she turned out the light, she checked Instagram again.

---

22 **out of sight** hidden – 25 **to go through sth** to experience sth difficult

The follow request from Mary Jessel was gone.

Thank god, she thought, and then she went to sleep.

The next morning, Linda awoke determined to help Wanda deal with her problem. The weight of her concerns about her past and her future had been lifted – at least temporarily – thanks to her talk with Hall. And all the drama connected to the picture of that sedan – whatever that had been about – seemed to have been handed off to the police. Now it was time for Wanda.

"I was hoping you had forgotten about that," Wanda said with a grimace, after Linda reminded her of their plan to speak with Mr. Adams. "But I forgot that you don't forget things."

They agreed that they would go immediately after their last class, when Mr. Adams would hopefully still be in his room. When the final bell rang, Linda went directly there, not even stopping at her locker, and found Wanda waiting for her in the hallway, looking anxious.

"You have to do the talking," Linda said. "I'm here for moral support, but it won't help your case if I talk for you."

Linda opened the door, and Wanda walked in in front of her.

Mr. Adams was an older man – not quite old, but older than most of the other teachers at their school. He tried to dress young – in polos, jeans and sneakers – but his '70s mustache and cheaply-dyed hair undermined his effort. He was sitting behind his desk and looked up when they came in, wearing an expression of curiosity.

"Hello, Wanda," he said. "Linda."

Linda had never taken Life Skills, but all the teachers knew her. She was a model student.

"What can I do for you?" he asked.

Linda hung back a bit, and Wanda stepped forward. Linda could see that her friend was trembling and started to wonder

---

5 **temporarily** for now, for a short time – 5 **thanks to** as a result of – 10 **grimace** an ugly facial expression – 17 **moral support** encouragement, advice – 22 **polo** short-sleeved cotton T-shirt with a collar – 23 **to undermine** to make sth weaker or less effective

if this idea of hers had been a bad one. She considered taking Wanda by the arm and fleeing, but it was too late now. They had to see it through.

"Mr. Adams," Wanda began. "I wanted to ask you about something."

"Okay," he said, leaning back in his chair. "Do you want to sit down?"

Wanda shook her head. Having taken a position about five feet in front of Mr. Adams's desk, she now seemed frozen in place.

"As you know," Wanda went on, "I'm not doing very well in your class. And if I don't do a little bit better, I'm not going to go to college in September."

"Why's that?"

"My college acceptance was conditional," she explained. "If I don't get a 3.25 this term, they're going to take my acceptance back. I'm doing well enough in my other classes, but this one is pulling me down."

"This one," Mr. Adams repeated, as if he found the phrasing curious. "This class is pulling you down."

"Yes," Wanda said, her nervousness suddenly increasing with the realization that she'd said something wrong. She'd already blown it.

Mr. Adams sat up, folding his arms on his desk.

"What can I do for you, Wanda?" he asked.

Wanda glanced over her shoulder at Linda, a questioning look. Linda replied with a short nod. Wanda turned back to face Mr. Adams.

"I was wondering…" Her voice trailed off. Her eyes seemed unfocused.

It was startling how quickly the small amount of confidence she had entered the room with had been annihilated. Even Mr.

---

2 **to flee** to run away – 3 **to see sth through** to complete sth you have started – 22 **to blow it** to miss an opportunity – 30 **startling** very surprising and worrying – 31 **to annihilate** to destroy completely

Adams seemed startled. He stood up and gestured toward a chair near the front of his desk, beckoning her to sit.

And suddenly Linda felt some relief: he wasn't cruel.

Wanda sat.

"What were you wondering?" Mr. Adams asked.

"I was wondering if–"

–there's some extra work I could do to improve my grade–

But instead of saying that, Wanda exhaled heavily, and all of her nervousness seemed to disappear.

"I was wondering how I ended up here. I'm not the smartest person in the world. I'm not even particularly smart. But I'm smart enough to get into Kendall."

Mr. Adams looked confused.

"That's my safety school," Wanda explained. "Or at least it was my safety school. Now even they don't want me. And all I've done all my life is what I was told to do. No one ever told me I was doing something wrong, even though clearly I was, because now I'm sitting here, one bad grade away from not going to college at all. And I'm not sure what I did wrong. Unless what I did wrong was not realize that no one was looking out for me. What I thought was right was wrong, at least for me. And now I'm sitting here hoping you'll help me, even though I don't deserve it, because I didn't do the work. I never took this class seriously because I didn't think I had to."

A heavy silence consumed the classroom.

Linda had gone from standing upright to leaning back against the closed classroom door. There had been a moment early on when she had been about to intervene. Now she was glad she hadn't. She had been stirred by her friend's revelation, and she had also related to it.

---

2 **to beckon** to signal with a gesture – 8 **to exhale** to breathe out – 25 **to consume** *(here)* to completely take over – 28 **to intervene** to interrupt with the aim of being helpful – 29 **stirred** moved emotionally – 29 **revelation** communication of sth that was unknown before – 30 **to relate to** to feel sth in common with, to understand

Wanda was steady, her eyes focused on the edge of Mr. Adams's desk. She seemed at peace with what she'd just realized, and just disclosed.

"Wanda," Mr. Adams said.

She looked at him, for the first time in a while.

"Hmm?"

"What can I do for you?"

"Nothing."

A few minutes later, out in the hallway, Wanda was walking slowly toward the exit. At her side, Linda was looking up, searching her friend's face for clues as to how she was feeling.

Finally, Wanda spoke.

"I feel like I just learned something," she said, "but too late for it to make any difference."

"Too late this time," Linda said. "But now you know."

"Yeah. But I forget things."

Linda nodded. With Wanda, there was no way of knowing if it would stick.

"So I guess I need to talk to my parents," Wanda said. "I told them I was accepted. I left out the conditionally part."

"Yikes."

Wanda stopped walking. Linda stopped too, and now they were facing each other.

"You need a hug?" Linda asked.

"I need a hug."

---

3 **to disclose** to share sth that had previously been private or secret – 18 **to stick** *(here)* to remain in sb's memory

And then Linda was holding Wanda – practically holding her up – and Wanda was crying so hard she was heaving.

Why was Linda trying to convince herself that the relationships she'd formed at high school were meaningless?

What is Mr Adams implying when he asks Wanda twice: 'What can I do for you?'?

Think about it...

Is protecting yourself from experiencing upsetting emotions always a bad thing? Think of some examples.

Friendship is important in life. What qualities do you appreciate most in your close friends?

Chapter 7

That was Tuesday. On Wednesday, nothing happened. Then on Thursday, Hall disappeared.

Or maybe he had disappeared on Wednesday. Because unusually he had not sent her a message at bedtime. And the message she'd sent him a couple of hours earlier had been received but, by the time she went to bed, had not been read. Two checks, but gray, not blue.

Thursday morning, nothing had changed. Linda resisted the urge to write to him again. Then in the parking lot at school, she saw that his car wasn't there, and he always arrived before her. Still, before the first bell rang, she passed by his homeroom. Maybe his car had broken down. Maybe his parents had driven him in. But when she passed by his homeroom, she saw that his desk was unoccupied.

In their group chat, she asked if anyone had seen or heard from Hall since the day before. No one had, and Hall did not appear in the chat. Everyone replied except him.

"So, what do you think happened?" Shaun asked, sounding more exasperated than curious.

School was over, and Linda was walking quickly to her car, with Shaun, Wanda and Christa a few steps behind her, struggling to keep up.

"I don't know," Linda answered. "I just know that something's wrong."

"But you seem so worried, Lin," Christa observed. "And he's just been offline all day."

"This has never happened before," Linda pointed out. "Never."

"Things are always happening that never happened before," Wanda said.

"This is different," Linda said. "This is Hall."

---

8 **to resist** *(here)* to stop yourself from doing sth – 9 **urge** a strong feeling or wish – 12 **homeroom** *(US Eng)* classroom – 14 **unoccupied** vacant – 19 **exasperated** annoyed – 22 **to struggle** to try hard to do sth

A few feet from her car, Linda pulled the key out of her purse and unlocked it. Her friends continued to follow her as she opened the driver's side door and climbed in behind the wheel. Wanda tapped on the window; Linda rolled it down.

"You want me to come with you?" Wanda asked.

"It's alright," Linda said. "I'm just going to go talk to his mom."

"Don't forget about the show," Christa said. "Starts at eight."

"I won't," Linda assured her. Then to Wanda she said, "Meet you here at seven thirty?"

"Yep."

Twenty minutes later, Linda was sitting on the living room sofa in Hall's house and his mother was setting a glass of water down in front of her.

"Hall wasn't at school today," Linda said as Hall's mother sat down across from her. "And he's been offline for the last twenty-four hours. I saw that his car's gone. Where is he?"

"We don't know. He left last night, and we don't know where he is."

"Have you tried calling him?"

"No point. His phone's right there."

Hall's mother looked to Linda's right, and Linda followed her gaze to an end table next to the sofa. Hall's phone was on it. She leaned over, picked it up and pressed the home button. It didn't unlock, but she could see the notifications: a dozen unanswered calls from her.

"You didn't ask him where he was going?" Linda said.

"We didn't see him leave."

"What have you done to try to find him?"

"Nothing," Hall's mother said with a shrug. "We often don't know where Hall is."

Linda studied Hall's mother's face for a moment. She hadn't expected this. She had expected either concern or an explanation, not this near apathy.

"I almost never don't know where Hall is," Linda said. "Something is wrong."

"I don't think anything is wrong, Linda. I'm his mother. If I thought something was wrong, I would do something."

Linda set Hall's phone down on the coffee table, next to the glass of water she hadn't touched.

"I think we should call the police," she said.

"Linda–"

"Something is wrong," Linda said, almost sternly. "And we should call the police."

Hall's mother sighed heavily, and then something in her face shifted.

"It must be wonderful," she said, "to be so young and sure of everything. So sure of your<u>self</u>. So sure that you know Hall and that you know something is wrong. Well, Linda, I don't want to deal with the police today, and neither does Hall's father. And if you decide to get them involved in our family's business, there will be consequences."

---

15 **apathy** lack of interest

The apathy that Linda had detected earlier had been replaced by a barely-contained rage. Somehow, without knowing how, Linda had pushed a button. She had come here out of concern for this woman's son, and now she was being threatened.

The front door opened and Hall's father walked in. He was wearing an expensive suit and tie and carrying a leather briefcase, which he set down in the foyer.

"Hi, Linda," he said as he moved into the living room. Sensing the tension, he asked, "Is everything alright?"

"Hall wasn't at school today, and Linda is concerned."

For an instant, Hall's father looked uneasy, then he smiled and looked at Linda.

"I'm sure everything is fine," he said.

"That all sounds very weird," Wanda said after Linda described her encounter with Hall's parents. "I thought Hall's mother liked you."

They were in the school theater, waiting for Christa's play to start. It was about fifteen minutes until curtain, and the theater was nearly full.

"Me too," Linda said. "But I felt so unwelcome in that house."

"So, what now?"

"I don't know. Whatever is going on, they don't want me to get involved. They clearly don't want me to call the police."

"Yeah, that was clear. Do you think Hall is alright?"

"I guess so?" Linda said in an uncertain tone. "I don't feel good about any of it, but his parents aren't worried, so why should I be? It's frustrating, though, that he doesn't have his phone. If he could just write, 'I'm fine, stay out of it,' I would be fine not knowing more."

"This has been a weird week," Wanda said. "I hope prom doesn't suck."

---

2 **barely-contained** only just controlled – 2 **rage** extreme anger – 4 **to threaten** to say that you will cause sb trouble in the future – 8 **to sense** to feel or understand without needing to be told – 9 **tension** a difficult and strained atmosphere – 15 **encounter** meeting – 22 **to get involved** to be included or mixed up in sth – 27 **frustrating** annoying

This reminded Linda of something. She checked the time.

"I'll be right back," Linda said, standing suddenly. She moved quickly down the row, moving sideways, apologizing as she bumped into people's knees. Reaching the end of the row, she turned and walked toward the stairs at the end of the stage. She went up the stairs and behind the curtain, and now she was backstage.

After a few minutes, she found Beth at the props table. She had a checklist in her hand and was making sure everything was ready to go.

"Beth," Linda said.

"Linda?" Beth said, clearly confused. "What are you doing back here? I mean, it's great to see you but–"

"I just have a quick question," Linda assured her. "Has Hall picked up his tux?"

"Not that I know of, but I don't work there during the week."

"Okay."

"I could call the store."

"Could you?"

"Right now?"

"It would just take a second, right?"

"Yeah, I guess," Beth conceded.

She took out her phone and turned it on.

"We've got to have them off backstage," she explained as her phone powered up.

"Sure."

Finally her phone was fully on and she called the tuxedo shop. After a brief conversation, she disconnected, shaking her head.

"No," she told Linda. "He hasn't."

Linda thought about this for a moment, leaving Beth standing awkwardly in front of her.

---

4 **to bump into** to knock against – 8 **props** the extra things needed for a stage performance – 22 **to concede** to agree reluctantly – 28 **to disconnect** to end a phone call

Finally, Beth said, "Look, I don't want to be rude, but–"

"I'm sorry," Linda said, snapping out of it. She glanced over her shoulder at the curtain. "Is there a way out of here that doesn't require me to go back onstage?"

"Sure," Beth said.

Linda watched the play in a state of distraction. It wasn't necessarily significant that Hall hadn't picked up his tux: he had forgotten to order it in the first place, so forgetting to pick it up was onbrand. But if he had – and in particular if he had today – then she would have been reassured. The fact that he hadn't left her concern unmitigated.

It was nearly ten-thirty when the play ended. Friends and family members of the cast and crew gathered in the cafeteria, where the tables had been folded up and pushed aside, for a modest opening night reception. When Christa found them, Linda and Wanda were standing near the entrance, clutching paper cups.

"So, what did you think?" she asked them.

"It was great," Linda said with a wide smile.

"It was strange," Wanda said bluntly. "You were fantastic, but the play was strange."

"Yeah, it's a strange play," Christa admitted.

"Why did the stage manager keep coming out? Was that supposed to happen?"

"That wasn't the real stage manager. That was a character."

"They should warn people about that," Wanda said. "It was confusing."

Suddenly, Linda got the sense that someone was looking at her, someone in front of her but at some distance. Looking away from Christa and toward the person, her eyes met the eyes of a man she didn't know, a man who instantly looked away.

---

6 **distraction** lack of attention – 11 **unmitigated** unchanged, in no way lessened – 13 **cast** actors in a play – 13 **crew** all the people involved in producing a play

It was not unusual for men to look at her, even men who were old enough to be her father. In fact, it was often men who were old enough to be her father.

But she knew instinctively that this man was not one of Hall's old perverts. This man had been looking at her differently, with something like worry in his eyes. And it was then that she knew, without the slightest doubt, that this was the man who had been in the sedan.

"Guys," she said to Wanda and Christa, interrupting them. "Don't look, and please smile. There's a man on the other side of the cafeteria. He's wearing a gray suit with a red tie, and what's left of his hair is kind of reddish-blond. Look at him, but do it casually, and not at the same time. Do either of you know him?"

After taking an inconspicuous look at him, Wanda said, "I don't know him."

Then Christa took a look and said, "That's the deputy mayor. My neighbor."

"Oh my god."

Although the deputy mayor's house was perched atop the Hill, it was Christa's house that was at the end of the road, which circled under the peak before it ended. This meant that on the way to Christa's, you passed by the steep driveway that led up to the deputy mayor's.

The sedan had been parked across from the entrance to the deputy mayor's driveway.

"His daughter is helping out with costumes," Christa was saying. "The funny thing is, when he came to rehearsal the first time, I didn't know who he was. He owns the house right next to me, and I see his wife and daughter all the time. But he says he's hardly ever there. He's got a farm east of town where he spends most of his time."

"A farm," Linda repeated. "East of town."

---

14 **inconspicuous** not obvious – 16 **deputy mayor** the second person in charge at the Town Hall – 19 **perched** placed or built high up on sth – 19 **atop** on the top of

The sedan had been found at a rest area about 100 miles east of town.

"How far away is it?" Linda asked.

"I don't know exactly," Christa said. "But I get the impression it isn't close."

"What's going on, Linda?" Wanda asked with a scrunched up expression.

"Can you come with me, Wanda? I need to go to this farm."

> How would you describe Hall's mother's reaction to Linda?

> What was significant about where the deputy mayor lived?

Think about it…

> How important to you is the ability to be in instant contact with friends and family? Would you find it difficult to live without that? Why?

> If you were in Linda's place, would you have the courage to pursue your suspicions as she is doing here?

---

6 **scrunched up** screwed up, worried

Chapter 8

"A lot of it isn't concrete," Linda said as they raced along the highway, headed east, "and the connections aren't all clear. But I'm feeling it all so strongly. My brain is just buzzing and it won't stop until I go to that farm and see if Hall is there."

"Why would the deputy mayor kidnap Hall?" Wanda asked.

"Because of that picture. If the man in that sedan was the deputy mayor, I don't think the woman he was with was his wife. I think it was the woman's car, not the man's."

"What happened to the woman?"

"Maybe we'll find her at the farm too."

It had not been too difficult for Wanda to find the location of the mayor's farm. He had been a public figure for decades, and he enjoyed presenting himself as a hard-working, relatable man of the earth, despite his enormous wealth. His farm – which was outside of town but still in the county, so not nearly as far away as the rest area – had been featured in many of his campaigns for office.

"Message from Christa," Wanda said, looking at her phone. "He just left."

They were operating on the assumption that his daughter would go home with her mother and that he would head straight for the farm. It had been twenty minutes since they'd left the school, so best-case scenario they had a twenty minute head start – maybe more, given how fast Linda was driving.

Wanda had looked at the farm on Street View and they had identified a point of entry. On the west side of the house, toward the back, there was a small staircase that led up to what they thought was probably the entrance to a kitchen. On either side of the door, there were two large, uncurtained windows so they could get a look inside.

They exited the freeway and drove past a closed gas station – the only sign of civilization. The road to the farm had no

---

13 **relatable** sb that people can identify with – 16 **to feature** to play an important role in sth – 16 **to campaign for office** to plan activities with a political aim – 22 **head start** a period of time ahead of sb else, e.g. in a race

streetlights, but the moon was out and full, so they could make out most of their surroundings. When they got to the farmhouse, they didn't stop. Instead they drove on about a half mile and parked on the side of the road. Hopefully the car was far enough up the road that the deputy mayor wouldn't see it if he arrived while they were still there.

"But that's not going to happen, right?" Wanda asked. "He's not going to arrive while we're still here?"

"He might," Linda said. "In which case we'll sneak out the back and head for the car."

"Are we making a bad decision?"

"Probably," Linda admitted. "Do you want to stay here?"

Wanda thought about it for a moment, then said, "No. I feel like I'd rather be with you than alone in a car in the dark in the middle of nowhere."

---

26 **to sneak out** to go out of a place secretly or without being seen

They moved slowly toward the farmhouse from the road, cell phone flashlights searching the ground for clear spots to place their feet. The sky was bright with moonlight, but the farmhouse yard was filled with tall pines, and the air was murky. The farmhouse was dark, but that didn't mean no one was inside, and they didn't want to step on a twig or a dry leaf and give themselves away.

They were moving diagonally across the yard, toward the west side. Halfway across, the yard was suddenly filled with light. A half dozen floodlights attached to the front of the house had come to life, replacing the murk with the equivalent of broad daylight. They froze, hoping that the lights had been triggered by motion detectors and not turned on manually by a living breathing human being who had actually seen them.

And then they saw the dog.

It had been standing on the front porch the entire time, concealed by the gloom. Now they saw it clearly, a large German Shepherd. Standing at attention, staring at them.

They looked at each other, the same question in their eyes: *What do we do now?*

Before they could react, the dog leapt off the porch and started sprinting toward them, barking angrily. Perhaps illogically, Linda started running in the direction they had been headed, toward the side of the house rather than back to her car. Wanda ran after her.

Linda rounded the corner of the house and looked over her shoulder, seeing Wanda round the corner just a few yards behind her. Then she saw the dog, rapidly closing the gap between itself and Wanda. Linda believed it would be mere seconds before the dog had one of Wanda's legs in its jaws.

Linda stopped and turned around, looking frantically left and right for something she could use as a weapon. But there was nothing. All she could do was watch.

Then the dog reached the end of its chain. Its head and neck stopped where they were, and so did its barking. Its body flew out in front of it, and it landed on its back, squirming on the ground for a long moment trying to right itself. When it finally got back on its feet, it looked stunned. Then the floodlights in the front yard went out – they had been set off by a motion detector after all – and the dog disappeared.

Now together, Linda and Wanda discovered that they were standing at the bottom of the set of five stairs leading up to the kitchen door.

"How much time do we have?" Wanda asked, breathing heavily.

Linda checked the stopwatch on her phone and said, "Sixteen minutes." Then she looked up at the door and asked, "I'm not sure that's even enough time to figure out how to get inside."

"Well then let's not waste time doing that."

---

4 **illogically** not very sensibly or rationally – 12 **jaws** an animal's mouth – 18 **to squirm** to move from side to side – 19 **to right yourself** to turn yourself the right way up – 20 **stunned** dizzy, confused

Wanda saw a large stone on the ground and picked it up. Then she climbed the stairs and threw it through the window to the left of the door, the same side the doorknob was on. The sound of breaking glass shattered the silence.

In two seconds, Linda was in front of the door next to Wanda.

"Sorry," Wanda said, "that dog made me a little bit crazy,"

Her arm was through the hole she'd made in the window, reaching for the doorknob.

"What if someone's inside?" Linda asked.

"No one's inside. That dog barking and the floodlights would've brought them out."

There was a click and Wanda brought her hand back out. Her other hand was on the doorknob. She tried turning it. It turned.

"Might be an alarm, though," she said, and then she pushed the door open.

They both waited and listened, but there was nothing. If there was an alarm, it was a silent one. They stepped into what was, after all, a kitchen.

"Okay." Linda looked at her phone. "We've got fourteen minutes to check every room." Linda took the first floor; Wanda went upstairs. Five minutes later, they met back in the kitchen.

"Anything?" Linda asked.

"Nothing," Wanda said.

"Me too," Linda sighed.

"There's a basement," Wanda said.

"I think we should check the basement together."

"Me too."

The door to the basement was in the kitchen. They opened it and pointed their cell phone flashlights down a simple wooden staircase that led to an unfinished basement. They saw stone walls and a dirt floor. They listened but heard nothing.

"We have eight minutes," Linda said.

---

3 **doorknob** a round handle for a door that you turn to open – 4 **to shatter** *(here)* to break the silence – 25 **basement** an area of a building below the ground floor

Wanda stepped forward and walked down the stairs. When she realized Linda wasn't following her, she stopped and turned.

"What?" Wanda asked.

"I'm just not sure what is happening with you."

"We can't leave this house until we search it. And I want to leave this house."

Wanda turned back and walked down the rest of the staircase. Linda followed her and soon they were standing together in the basement.

It was an open, empty space, clearly not used for storage. They shone their flashlights around, but there was nothing to see. Until Linda noticed that the far wall was made of wood.

"The basement is smaller than the house, isn't it," Linda said.

Wanda looked up and thought for a moment about the space she'd just been in.

"I think so," she said.

"So then either the basement is just smaller than the house," Linda said, "or that wall is fake and there's a secret room behind it."

Wanda walked up to the wall and hit it. It was paneling, flimsy and cheap. If there was a secret room behind it, it had been made hastily.

Linda walked the length of the wall, running her hand along it. Finally she found a seam. She slipped her fingertips into it, grabbed, and pulled. A section of paneling came loose and fell to the floor. They had found the entrance. They stepped up to it and looked inside.

The room was pitch dark. The windows had been blacked out, so no moonlight could get in. They pointed their cell phones inside.

---

10 **storage** keeping things that are not currently in use – 18 **fake** false – 20 **paneling** thin sheets of board – 20 **flimsy** not strong, bad quality – 24 **seam** the line where two pieces join together – 25 **to grab** to take hold of sth – 28 **pitch dark** with no light at all – 28 **to black out** to put material across a window to stop any light coming in

"Oh."

"God."

The only furniture in the room was a mattress, placed against the far wall on the dirt floor. The mattress itself was bare, and there was no pillow. A few sheets were on the mattress, dirty and balled up.

A heavy-duty metal ring had been screwed into the wall. Attached to the ring was one end of a thick chain. Attached to the other end of the chain was a shackle – a shackle that was around the ankle of a woman who was very obviously dead.

"I think we need to leave now," Wanda said. There was wooziness in her voice.

The woman was on her front, sprawled across one corner of the mattress, her hips on it, her legs and her face in the dirt. Linda wondered if this was the woman she had seen in that sedan on the Hill five days before. She wondered how long she had suffered and when she had died. And then Linda realized that if this woman could die in this house, then she and Wanda could too.

She checked her stopwatch. Four minutes.

She stepped into the secret room. The smell was astonishing. She stood over the woman and took several photos with her phone, checking to make sure the flash was doing its job and they were in focus. Then she rejoined Wanda.

She sent the photos to the group chat, along with this message:
Found this in the basement of the deputy mayor's farmhouse. Make sure pics get seen.

Wanda saw the message appear on her phone.

"Are we going now?" she asked.

"We are going now," Linda said.

Stepping into the kitchen, they realized that there was light coming from the front of the house. Leaning into the hallway that

---

6 **balled up** messily screwed into a ball – 7 **heavy-duty** not easily damaged, strong –
7 **to screw sth into sth** to fix sth in place – 9 **shackle** metal ring for a prisoner's foot
– 9 **a shackle** that was around the ankle of a woman who was very obviously dead. –
12 **wooziness** faintness, dizziness – 23 **to rejoin** to go back to sb

led to the living room, they saw that the front yard floodlights were on. The front yard was as bright as daylight. And the dog wasn't barking.

Linda looked at her stopwatch: two minutes.

"He drove even faster than I did," she said.

They heard the unmistakable sound of keys turning a lock. He was at the front door.

"Let's go," Wanda said, moving toward the kitchen door.

Linda followed her, and in seconds they were outside.

"Around the back," Linda said.

They would avoid the front yard this time, and its floodlights, and its dog. They would move, undetected, through the wooded area on the house's east side and come out on the road just a few yards away from Linda's car. It was perfect unless there were floodlights in the back yard as well.

Unfortunately there were floodlights in the back yard as well. And almost as soon as they went on, exposing them in the middle of the yard, the back door crashed open and the deputy mayor was there. This time, however, they didn't stop, as they had with the dog. This time they sprinted around the corner of the house and into the trees, making a beeline for Linda's car.

Racing out of the trees and into the road, Linda already had her keys out, unlocking the doors. Wanda was a few steps behind her. When the deputy mayor emerged from the trees, already red-faced and sweaty, they were almost to the car, and it seemed almost impossible that he would ever catch them. So he decided to shoot at them instead.

Linda was at the car when the shooting started. She got in behind the wheel, and in seconds Wanda was in the seat next to her. Linda started the car and stepped on the gas, not thinking about the fact that she didn't know what was in this direction, just assuming that the road led somewhere.

---

6 **unmistakable** obvious – 12 **undetected** not seen or found – 21 **to make a beeline for** to head directly for

And then the road ended, soon and abruptly. She stopped in front of the barrier. Beyond it was a river.

"He knows this road doesn't go anywhere," Linda said.

"So he's still back there," Wanda said.

"But that's the way we have to go."

"So then that's the way we go."

Linda turned the car around and again stepped on the gas. Moments later, he was in front of them, waiting for them, standing in the center of the road, looming in their headlights.

He raised his gun and took aim.

"Pass him close on the left," Wanda said.

"His left?"

"Your left."

"Okay."

---

17 **abruptly** suddenly – 26 **to take aim** to point gun a sb/sth

He started firing, and they both ducked. Linda gave the car more gas and veered slightly to the left. Wanda leaned back, put her feet against her door – and shoved it open.

The door hit almost all of him. The window shattered.

Wanda pulled her legs back in. The door slammed shut.

As they raced away, they looked back and saw him on the ground, several yards from where he'd been standing. Moving, alive, but not going anywhere. He was in the same place when the police arrived.

In the hospital, he admitted everything.

The woman in the basement had been his employee – and his lover. He had been promising to leave his wife but had never done it, so she had gone to his house that Saturday to do what she had been threatening to do for years: reveal their relationship to his wife. By chance, he had been there and had seen her car outside. What Linda had seen that night had been a fight, not a makeout session.

Things escalated. The woman tried to kill herself by smashing her hand through the window of her car and cutting her wrist. He stopped her and took her to his farmhouse. She seemed out of control, so he created a secret room in his basement and locked her up in it, not knowing what damage she would do if he didn't. She found a way to kill herself anyway – probably by using something she had stashed in her purse – so he moved her car to a rest area in a different county and removed anything that would've allowed anyone to identify the owner.

When he saw Linda at opening night, he recognized her from that night on the Hill, and it occurred to him that she might recognize him. So he became nervous, and even though she didn't recognize him, his nervousness gave him away.

---

1 **to duck** to lower your head of body to avoid sth, e.g. a bullet – 2 **to veer** to turn slightly – 3 **to shove** to push with force – 4 **to shatter** *(here)* to break into small pieces – 5 **to slam** to shut with force – 14 **to reveal** to tell sb sth that was secret – 28 **to occur to sb** to suddenly realize – 30 **to give sb away** to betray, to make your secret obvious

He said he didn't know where Hall was. Didn't even know who Hall was. Didn't know anything about who had viewed Hall's Instagram stories. Or the account that had sent Linda a friend request. He said he didn't really know anything about Instagram at all.

The name Mary Jessel rang a bell, though.

"Isn't that the name of the governess?" he asked. "In The Innocents?"

The car door Wanda had shoved at him had done a lot of harm. He was struggling to breathe. Most of what he had said before had come out garbled, but those questions had come out clear.

"I love that movie. You watch it and think you know what happened. But you don't."

> What gave the girls a clue about the existence of a secret room?

> The deputy mayor was armed but the girls weren't. How did they manage to escape from him?

Think about it...

> What do we normally assume about people who hold an official position? Describe some characteristics that we would expect to see.

> Does the last sentence in Chapter 8 sum up the story for you so far? Do you think there are any more surprises to come?

---

6 **to ring a bell** to sound familiar, to remind sb of sb/sth – 7 **governess** a woman who looks after and teaches young children – 8 **innocent** sb who has done nothing wrong (*The Innocents* – a Nordic horror film, 2021) – 11 **garbled** confused, difficult to understand

Chapter 9

Prom. At a hotel in town. The theme had something to do with Paris, which most of them had visited but none of them knew anything about.

Linda was at the entrance, waiting for Hall, who Beth had informed her had picked up his tuxedo the previous day. She had still not heard from him directly, but she also knew that he hadn't been home yet. According to his father, his phone was still in their living room, drained of power. Yet she almost didn't believe he would appear.

And then there he was, marching up the steps toward her, looking sheepish.

He stopped a few steps below her, looked up at her.

"So," he said.

"No. I'm going to try not to be angry at you. But two days ago, I broke into a crazy person's house looking for you. So I need more than 'so.'"

---

24 **drained of power** *(here)* having no battery power – 27 **sheepish** embarrassed

"Can I point out that we both look great?"
"Yes you can."
"We both look great."
"You look alright."
"I deserve that."
"You deserve worse."

Hall couldn't hold back anymore. He moved to the top step and wrapped his arms around her. Behind them, music was playing, and people were enjoying themselves.

"I'm so sorry, Linda," Hall said. He pulled back and looked at her. "You and I talked about doing something <u>now</u>. So I did something now. And it didn't go well."

"You told them," Linda said. "That explains a lot."

"Yeah I told them," he said. "And me being gay became something else for them to fight about. So I left and went to my uncles' place. And I was almost glad that I couldn't tell you about it, because I know that you've got your own talk coming up."

"But?"

"But that was a huge mistake. And I'm sorry."

"Apology accepted."

She hooked one of her arms into one of his, and turned him around. They stood facing the entrance.

"I don't know what's going to hit my parents harder," she said. "The fact that I'm gay, or the fact that I don't want to get an MBA anymore."

"Your parents?" Hall said. "Definitely the MBA."

"You're probably right," she said. "By the way, we need to talk about Wanda."

"Okay."

Then they went inside and danced.

---

7 **to hold back** to stop yourself

> Why had Hall 'disappeared' for a short time?

> What did Linda have to talk to her own parents about?

Think about it...

Were you expecting the 'twist' at the end of the story? How did it make you feel?

Are you good at handling difficult conversations? What advice would you give – to yourself or to someone else – about how to approach such a situation?

Activities

Focus on the story

1. Are the sentences True or False?
Tick the correct box.

		True	False
1.	Linda's friends had a drink waiting for her when she arrived at Christa's.	☐	☐
2.	Shaun was looking forward to the school prom.	☐	☐
3.	At the tuxedo shop, Beth gave Hall a tux she had ready for him.	☐	☐
4.	Linda was good academically and had a university lined up to go to.	☐	☐
5.	Someone called Mary Jessel tried to follow Wanda on Instagram.	☐	☐
6.	When the brown sedan was found, there wasn't much glass anywhere despite the broken window.	☐	☐
7.	Shaun suggested telling the police about the photo Linda had taken of the car.	☐	☐
8.	Hall and Linda both came from financially well-off backgrounds.	☐	☐
9.	Mr Adams was a young teacher who was popular with the students.	☐	☐
10.	Wanda admitted that she had done little work in Mr Adams' class.	☐	☐
11.	Hall was quite often late arriving at school in the morning.	☐	☐
12.	Hall had not been in contact with Linda for a couple of days.	☐	☐
13.	Linda recognized the deputy mayor when he came to see the show.	☐	☐
14.	Linda thought that Hall might be at the farmhouse.	☐	☐
15.	If the dog hadn't been chained up, he would have attacked the girls.	☐	☐

2. What happened when?

Put the events in the correct order (1-10). Write the number in the correct box below.

a. A sedan was found at a rest area with a smashed window.
b. Hall goes missing.
c. Hall reappears.
d. Linda and Hall start getting notifications from unknown contacts.
e. Linda goes to the school play and sees a suspicious man.
f. Linda visits Hall's house.
g. The friends identify the sedan as the same one as in the photo.
h. The friends tell the authorities about the car.
i. The photo of the sedan is put on social media.
j. Wanda and Linda make a discovery at the farmhouse.

a	b	c	d	e	f	g	h	i	j
								1	

3. What did they look like?

Complete the descriptions of these places with words from the box.

| ceilings | couch | courts | edifice | field | floodlights |
| flutes | island | lake | pines | porch | treeless |

1 The Hill: It had a 1 _____ top. Parts of the Hill faced the 2 _____ .
2 The farmhouse: There were 3 _____ in the yard and a large dog on the 4 _____ . There were 5 _____ at the front and at the back.
3 The school: It had a nice grassy 6 _____ that belonged to the campus where they could sit and chat. It also had tennis 7 _____ .
4 Christa's place: In the living room, there was a 8 _____ , a loveseat and champagne 9 _____ on the coffee table. The kitchen had a useful 10 _____ in the middle.
5 The shopping mall: It was – or could have been – quite an impressive 11 _____ . The 12 _____ were high and the place echoed. Unfortunately, it was not doing well.

4. How did you like it?

Reflect on the story and complete the review form.

What I liked

1.

2.

3.

What I didn't like

1.

2.

3.

My favorite character is _____ because:

My favorite chapter is _____ because:

Overall, I **would / would not** recommend this story because:
_____

Stars: _____ / 5

☆☆☆☆☆

Focus on the people

1. What is Linda like? And you?

Which of the adjectives in the box would you use to describe Linda?

> aggressive ambitious caring competent
> courageous down-to-earth forgetful
> jealous patient practical reliable
> responsible shy trustworthy

Now write down 7-10 adjectives you could use to describe yourself.

2. Qualities of friendship

One theme running throughout *The Sedan* is friendship. How do the group of friends help each other out? Give at least one example from the story for each of the friends: Christa, Linda, Wanda, Shaun and Hall.

Who?	What?
Christa	
Linda	
Wanda	
Shaun	
Hall	

Focus on grammar

1. The passive

Use the past perfect passive of the verb given to complete the sentences. Each sentence must be true according to the story. Look at the example given.

1 By the end of the story, we understand that the floodlights outside the farmhouse **hadn't been turned on** (turn on) manually.
2 The photo on Hall's account of the sedan ……………………………………….. (take) by himself.
3 On the Hill, trees ………………………………….. (cut down) so that houses could be built.
4 Hall regretted that at least some of the money from the federal government ………………………………………….. (spend) on improving the Southeast Village shopping mall.
5 When the sedan was found, one of its windows ……………………………………….. (break).
6 Video footage …………………………………………. (use) during the investigation into the possible crime.
7 After the crime, the sedan ……………………………………….. (abandon) in the Hill.
8 At the farmhouse, an extra small room ……………………………………. (build) in the basement.

2. Prepositional phrases

Complete the prepositional phrases taken from the story, now presented in a different context. Choose the correct preposition from the box to complete the phrase. There is one extra preposition.

| by | for | in | of | on | to | with |

1 The US state of Massachusetts is **famous ....** its universities, especially Harvard.
2 Sue and John split up after they discovered that they really had **nothing .... common**.
3 Oliver tried really hard to get his head around the laws of physics but it was **............ no avail**.
4 They all felt there was **no point ....** going on a picnic when the weather was so cold and wet.
5 How far is a child's character **determined ....** the situation in which they grow up?
6 The store was dark and quiet. They were **............ the threshold** about to go in when suddenly a gun was aimed at them.
7 She was widely praised for helping the victim **instead ....** running away.
8 The main complaint was that there was **nothing .... do** in the town for the young people.

Build your vocabulary

Focus on words

1. Similar but different
Circle the correct word in each sentence.
1. In the end, the detectives **concealed / concluded** that there was not enough evidence to send the attacker to prison.
2. The crime writer had **anticipated / allocated** that she would spend six months to finish the novel but in fact it took double that time!
3. The sun was so bright that day that we had to **squeeze /squint** in order to look at our mobile phones.
4. Nathaniel wanted to study criminology and he r**evoked / resisted** any attempt to make him change his mind.
5. However many times you tell me, you're never going to **convince / confirm** me that she is a thief!
6. My sister seems to have perfected the art of **shoving / slamming** the door loudly whenever she leaves the room after an argument.

2. Word formation
Complete the sentences with the correct form of the word in brackets. Add a negative prefix (dis-, in-, mis-, un-) and make any other necessary changes.

1. There's an _____ rule in our house that everyone has to tidy up the kitchen after they use it. (write)
2. They exchanged a few words and then she _____ the phone. She didn't have the time to argue about silly things. (connect)
3. His French accent was _____ – I knew it was Alain as soon as I heard him. (mistake)
4. Do let me know if that date is _____ for our meeting and I can easily change it. (convenient)
5. Sylvia always felt it was a _____ to have been born the fifth out of five children since she was always treated as the 'baby' of the family. (fortune)
6. The murder went _____ for ten years! (detect)

The Sedan – the mind map

You can add any words to this mind map from the glossary or from the story for your own learning.

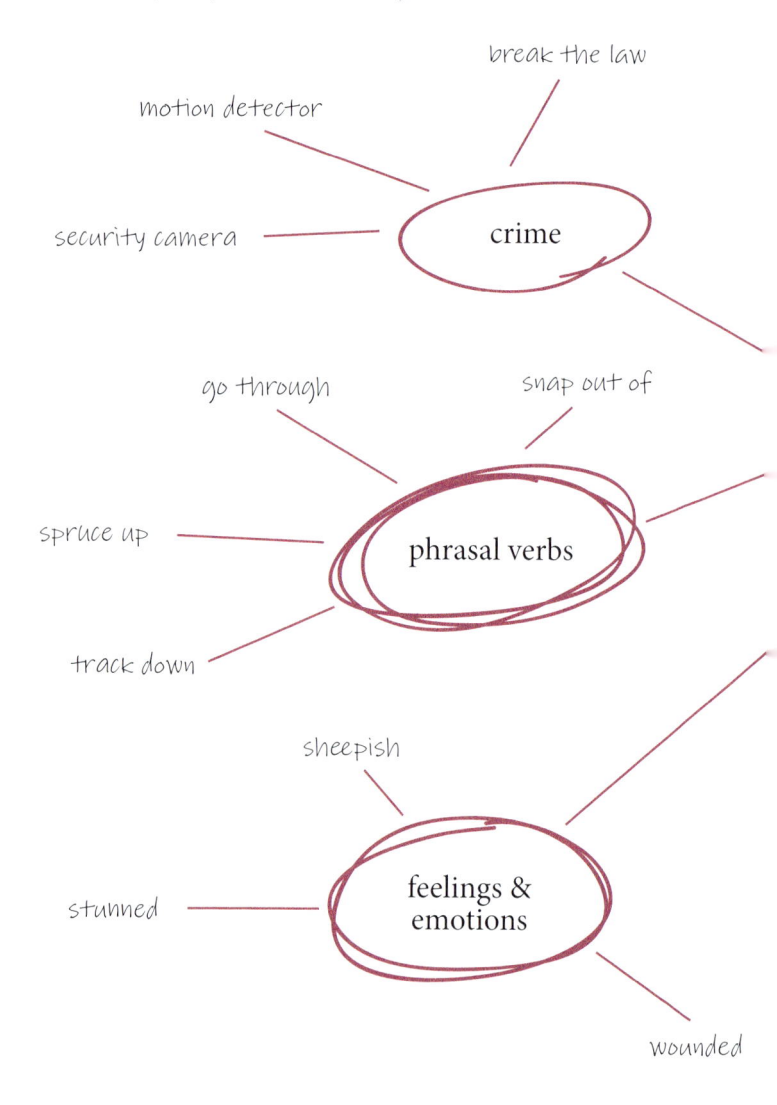

crime
- break the law
- motion detector
- security camera

phrasal verbs
- go through
- snap out of
- spruce up
- track down

feelings & emotions
- sheepish
- stunned
- wounded

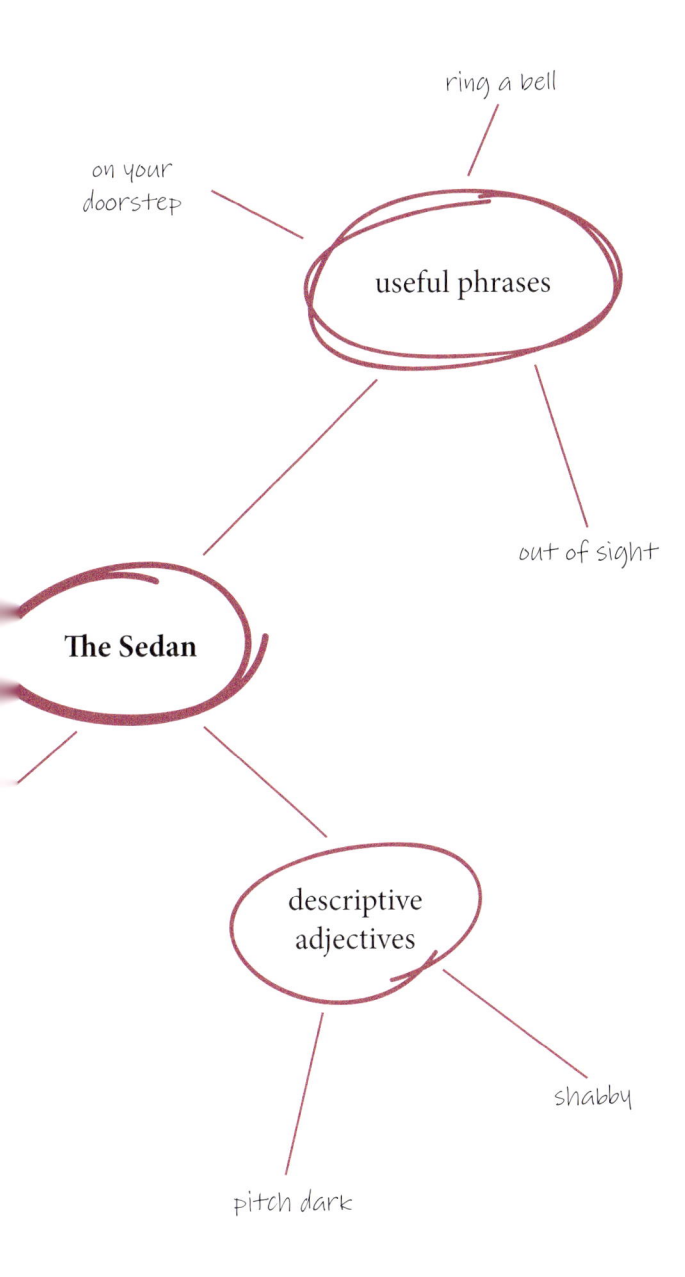

The Sedan

useful phrases
- ring a bell
- on your doorstep
- out of sight

descriptive adjectives
- shabby
- pitch dark

Glossary

	New word?	Notes / connected words

Crime
- admit ☐
- against the law ☐
- alarm ☐
- break the law ☐
- bribe ☐
- call the police ☐
- case ☐
- floodlights ☐
- footage ☐
- gun ☐
- identity ☐
- investigator ☐
- motion detector ☐
- security camera ☐
- shooting ☐
- state police ☐
- take aim ☐
- weapon ☐

Descriptive adjectives
- agape ☐
- cavernous ☐
- murky ☐
- pitch dark ☐
- shabby ☐
- uncurtained ☐
- unmown ☐
- unoccupied ☐

	New word?	Notes / connected words

Feelings / Emotions
- exasperated ☐
- frustrating ☐
- harried ☐
- ironic ☐
- sheepish ☐
- skeptical ☐
- startling ☐
- stirred ☐
- stunned ☐
- unsympathetic ☐
- wounded ☐

Phrasal verbs
- go through ☐
- hold back ☐
- make out ☐
- see sth through ☐
- set sth aside ☐
- snap out of ☐
- split up ☐
- spruce up ☐
- stumble across ☐
- take in ☐
- tear down ☐
- track down ☐
- turn down ☐

Phrases
- make a beeline for ☐
- on your doorstep ☐
- out of control ☐

Find out more

Find out more

1.

1 Choose a crime author either that you particularly like or who is well-known and look them up on the Internet. What advice do they give about writing crime novels? Make a note of what they say below.

1
2
3
4
5

2 Do you think that crime and suspense fiction is popular these days? Give your reasons below.

Yes, because …	No, because …

3 What do you think are the most important characteristics of a good crime novel? Write down some words in your language that you would use to talk about this subject. Find out the meaning of the words you have written in English.

crime novels	
Words in my language	Words in English

Answer key

Focus on the story
Questions at the end of each chapter

Chapter 1
- They are trying to approach an isolated house and try and see what or who was inside.
- The floodlights came on; they saw a large dog that was defending the property.

Chapter 2
- The Hill is now obviously an area where wealthy residents live and therefore its status is high and well-respected.
- Hall had left getting his tuxedo till the last minute, and she thought that it might not be ready in time with the correct colors to match her dress.

Chapter 3
- The reasons were that its situation was inconvenient for people from the town, it was shabby and it was difficult to get to.
- Linda means that they both needed the physical exercise.

Chapter 4
- She wasn't doing well in one essential subject, Life Skills. If she failed that, she wouldn't get the grades required by the only university that had given her an offer.
- Linda suggests that Wanda should talk to the Life Skills teacher about the problem.

Chapter 5
- There was blood on the seat and the door; there had been attempts to remove any personal 'evidence' i.e. personal items, the license plates and the VIN number.
- Linda is worried about the differences between being rich and poor and how this situation never seems to improve. Also,

she feels that there is in-build prejudice in society against anyone who is not a straight white male.

Chapter 6
- So that the pain of leaving her friends wouldn't be so strong.
- Mr Adams is implying that a) the problem is Wanda's and not his, and b) no way would he every consider doing anything 'illegal' to help her out.

Chapter 7
- Defensive and unwilling to enter into any dialogue with Linda.
- The sedan was parked opposite his house.

Chapter 8
- The difference in size between the basement and the house above it.
- They got in the car and drove it right next to him. Wanda opened the car door which hit the deputy mayor with force, enough to injure him seriously.

Chapter 9
- He had told his parents he was gay. They had obviously been negative about it so he'd gone to stay with his uncles.
- Linda had to tell her parents that she was gay and also that she didn't want to study for an MBA.